Seven Biblical Principles of Success

Dameon Gibbs

GPC
GIBBS PUBLISHING
CONGLOMERATE

ISBN: 978-1-966856-14-6

"You will never possess what you are unwilling to pursue,"

Bishop Clarice Fluitt

Acknowledgment

In every case, I first give thanks to my Lord and Savior Jesus the Christ. Without Him none of this would be possible. Jesus' blood, Spirit, and Word have forever changed me, granting me a life that I never thought possible.

I wish to thank my best friend and wife, Tiffany Gibbs, for her continuous support of me and my goals through all the long nights.

I give special thanks to my pastors Donald and Judith Peart for being my spiritual mentors and parents. May God continue to bless you with all spiritual blessings.

And last but not least, I would like to thank all my friends and family that have supported me through this long process. God bless you all.

Table of Contents

Preface

Identifying with the I AM
Ps.139:14

"I will praise thee; for I am fearfully *and* wonderfully made: marvellous *are* thy works; and *that* my soul knoweth right well."

This scripture is a favorite for many, yet, I think it's still a hard one for a lot of us to truly grasp.

It says [inserting words from Hebrew definition], "I am made with reverence and distinction: distinguished and great deed or product, and my soul wholly knows by seeing or observation." By seeing yourself, you know that everything God fashions, is to be respected and is distinct. Meaning, we are to respect ourselves and others in our differences because it was God's intention to make us this way. 2 Corinthians 10: 12 (NIV) states, "We do not dare to classify or compare ourselves with some who commend themselves. When they measure themselves by themselves and compare themselves with themselves, they are not wise." The Bible clearly states, to compare ourselves to others shows a lack of wisdom or understanding, as it is stated in other translations. Understanding of what, you may ask? The distinct work we are in God, with a distinct function and place. And if we believe we are made in God's image [see Gen. 1:26], then why do we struggle so much?

More than likely, at least I can say for me, it is because of words spoken over me, the wrong words. In pushing toward attaining goals, I have battled over past things spoken over me, indicating I would fail or did not have what was needed to succeed. And if you are like me and someone or maybe people over time told you enough wrong things about yourself, you may have never had the chance to identify yourself with the I

1

AM, God. God in turn, must be given the opportunity to heal us by telling us who we REALLY are. We are first, 1)His. 2)We are made in His similitude. 3)When we accept Jesus as Lord and Savior, we are no longer intrinsically wrong, we are made right. 4)We are lovely to Him [see Songs of Solomon] and 5)We are so precious to Him, He knows the number of hairs on our heads [Luke 12:7].

Words are so powerful; the world was created by them. Jesus is the Word of God. Let us begin to speak the right words, words of truth and life over ourselves, our lives, and others. Replace the "you can't" with "I can" turn the "you won't" into "you will." Proverbs 23:7 (KJV) says, "For as he thinketh in his heart, so is he..." That phrase, "for as he thinketh" means literally to split or open, reason out, calculate, to act as a gate keeper, to estimate. Your thoughts literally act as a gate keeper or estimator of your life. Let us think positive thoughts.

Know it right well - you are worthy of respect, and you are a work of art, distinguished among your brethren. I pray healing for us all from the bad words and curses spoken over our persons and life, in Jesus' name. Let us speak positive words and move forward into success in God's purpose for our lives.

Tiffany Gibbs

Forward

Before we dive into this book, I want to tell you a little about myself. I am one of five children born to Willie and Carnita Gibbs. I was born and raised in Baltimore City, Maryland. We lived the typical life of inner-city kids growing up in the late 70s, 80s and early 90s. Yes, our neighborhoods were filled with drugs and violence, but that did not stop us from having fun and living a good life.

Although my parents worked hard to provide for us, we were still considered a statistical number in the eyes of the government — a number that was bound to continue the cycle of being on drugs, welfare, alcoholism, and overall failure. However, God thought differently and decided to change and break that chain in 1998 when I accepted His Son. It was then that He changed the course of my life, placing me on a path of success as long as I kept Him as my Head.

I remember the day He first ministered His salvation to me. I was sixteen years old, it was a warm summer night, and I had just arranged with a childhood friend to purchase a few pounds of marijuana to sell. To celebrate my arrangement, I went to the bar and bought two pints of Jack Daniels for myself. After drinking both bottles, I found myself walking down a dark street alone thinking of my future success. I was in my own world, dreaming of all the money that would soon be coming my way. It was my world, well at least that is what I thought. Lo and behold, I ran into another good friend of mine, who spoke life-changing words to me that night, on that lonely dark street; words that I will never forget.

After talking about random things, he finally spoke to me what the Lord placed on his heart. His words were *"a drunken man cannot inherit the Kingdom of God,"* (see **1 Cor. 6:9-10**). Hearing those words stung like a thousand needles to my soul, as I grew up in a church-going household that believed. And even with all my wrongdoings, like many, I still believed that I was Heaven bound. But the Lord's word checked my life that night. That night I vowed to visit my friend's church the following Sunday for service. I did and later dedicated my life to the Lord. My life was forever changed.

I say this because my life went from a life without a vision, to a life with one. I had been a sixteen-year-old boy selling drugs with workers twice my age, extorting people for monies due, while my parents believed I was an innocent teenager. However, the Lord saw all my vices and saw fit to intervene. He changed me from an illegal businessperson to a legal businessperson.

And just as I went full throttle after the drug game, I changed my life and went full throttle after God. I never looked back, and I never went back to meet up with my friend to purchase those few pounds of marijuana. What makes this story more powerful, is that several years later that same friend that I was supposed to buy drugs from was brought up on federal kingpin charges for possession. There is no telling if I would have been caught up or not, but I like to think the Lord saved me from such a life. To this day, the majority of my friends from that era are either in jail, dead, or are living the same life they did nearly twenty years ago.

It was in my new state of my salvation that the Lord begin to speak well over me, giving my life a vision, purpose, and direction. In the year 1999, He began telling me that I would attend college, and that I would write several books. What you are reading is my twenty-second book. He also told me I would own several properties. My wife and I currently own three properties. Furthermore, He supernaturally began removing those people that were not conducive to His vision for my life, while adding those that were.

I did not share this to boast of myself, but to boast in the Lord. Showing how He can take the lowest of people in society and bring them to a place where they are successful in Him. He can take misused talents and redirect them for good. I am a living witness that the Lords' words never fail, what He says always comes to pass. We as believers must learn to keep faith and trust in Him through all situations. I continue to run after the promises and words He has spoken over me, and I pray that you do the same. May this word encourage and bring you comfort. Never stop chasing after your visions and dreams, know that they are yours until your last breath. If He can do it for me, He surely can do it for you.

Introduction

God wants all of His people to be successful, spiritually and physically. He has given us a written guideline and format to help bring about that success. The purpose of this book was not to suggest the gaining of physical wealth by any means, although I believe that an attribute of success in Christ can be physical wealth. This written work will focus on success as a whole; successful minds, spirituality, our bodies, families and, for some, financial wealth.

Before one can continue reading this book, one must know that this is not a prosperity message or pyramid scheme. This book is built on the foundation of Jesus Christ, with the sole purpose being to build up confidence in God's people which is every human being, teaching them that there is success without wealth. Principle is defined as a rule or basic generalization accepted as true and which can be used as a basis for reasoning or conduct. It is from this thought that I chose the title of this book because I did not wish to confuse people with false teachings of fast wealth. Instead I desired functional concepts taken from the Bible, that if applied properly I believe could lead the body to success in all things over time.

To properly understand the meaning of Biblical success, we must first define success in modern terms. Webster's Dictionary defines success as a degree or measure of succeeding, favorable or desirable outcome: the attainment of wealth, favor and eminence (lit. a position of prominence or superiority). It amazes me how these aspects are all qualities that our Lord and Savior possess. Jesus the Christ was and is successful in all things that He set out to accomplish. The Father had a desirable outcome for Him that He met, He has favor, the attainment of all wealth is His, and He has the pre-eminence in all things.

Paul the Apostle wrote in **Colossians 1:18-19**, *"And he (Christ) is the head of the body, the church: who is the beginning, the firstborn from the dead that in all (lit. whatsoever, whosoever, the whole) thing, he might have the preeminence. For it pleased the Father that in Him should all fullness dwell."*[1] Because of the Father's willingness to place preeminence in Jesus, the Father's will for His creation was fulfilled or completed in Christ. Fullness is defined as repletion or completion, what fills, what is filled (as container, performance, period).[2]

So, in essence, we find success or completion in Christ Jesus when we keep Him as our head. Keeping Him as our head, we gain the same attributes that He possesses, whether it is favor, eminence, a measure of succeeding or the attainment of wealth. **Eph. 3:6** reads, *"That the Gentiles should be (lit. to exist) Fellow heirs, and of the same body, and partakers of his promise (lit. divine assurance) in Christ by the gospel,"* KJV.

God is a God of thoughtful planning. He does nothing haphazardly, especially when it comes to His creation. We are not an accidental thought when God was bored one day. No, we are made with a purpose and for a purpose. **Jeremiah 1: 4-5** reads, *"Then the word of the Lord came unto me, saying, Before I formed[3] thee in the belly I knew[4] thee, and before thou camest forth out of the womb I sanctified thee, and I ordained thee a prophet unto the nations."* The Lord knows us through the formation in the womb. The Lord knows us and our talents.

---

[1] see **Col. 1:18-19**
[2] See Strgs#4138
[3] form = squeezing into shape, mold, fashion [Strgs#3335]
[4] know = to know by seeing and designation [Strgs#3045]

When we accept Christ as being the head of our body, we immediately become fellow-heirs and partakers of His divine assurance. It is from that moment that He begins to make us complete. This book will only serve to highlight seven principles of how we are complete in Him and being complete we are heirs to the promise, and that promise being success.

To learn of these seven principles, we will be examining the Book of Genesis. It is in the Book of Genesis that we first witness God being successful when creating, and we get a glance at the various steps He took to reach that success with each of the seven creation days. I will be analyzing and breaking down each of the creation days, describing how each day can be applied to our lives now. And how we can use it as a guideline for our life when reaching for the same success. The Lord wants all of His creation to be successful, and His word, Son and Spirit are the best means of obtaining it. However, we must keep in mind that success does not necessarily equate to wealth as we will come to read and as society wants us to believe.

Day One

*"The only thing worse than being blind
is having sight but no vision."*

Hellen Keller

Day One
Let the Vision Shine

Genesis 1:1-5 KJV:

1. In the beginning, God created the heaven and the earth.
2. And the earth was without form and void, and darkness was upon the face of the deep. And the Spirit of God moved upon the face of the waters.
3. And God said, let there be light: and there was light.
4. And God saw the light, that it was good: and God divided the light from the darkness.
5. And God called the light Day, and the darkness he called Night. And the evening and the morning were the first day.

Here in **Genesis 1:1-5**, we see God take the first step towards the principle of success. And that step is recognizing or seeing the potential of that which is good. Then immediately separating the good from the bad.

In the beginning or the first-fruit and principal thing[1], God created both heaven and earth, and during that process He said, "let there be light." Said is the Hebrew word *"amar"*, meaning "to say, command, appoint, charge, publish, promise and determine [2]." After creating, He commanded and charged the light to come forth, and

> *"Vision is the art of seeing what is invisible to others."*
>
> *-Jonathan Swift*

---

[1] see Strgs#7225
[2] See Strgs#559

once it did He saw that it was good. "Good" is defined as "well, beautiful, cheerful, precious.[1]"

When God created, He saw beauty and cheerfulness in what He had created. He recognized the good which came out of Him, for the light that was created, was created from the very words released from Him. We as a people must operate in the same manner, grasping the idea of the light. We must recognize all the good, beautiful, cheerful, and precious things that God has placed within us and how He wants us to speak and release that beautiful thing out into the world.

A vision board is a collage of images, picture, and affirmations of ones dreams and desires to serve as a source of inspiration and motivation, and to use the law of attraction to attain goals.

Now I want you to visualize the light as being an idea or even a talent. It is that light bulb that goes off in our head when we have a new creative idea. Anyone that is in any creative field, will tell you that it is a beautiful thing to create. In this case, the light is your vision and goal.

So when you have or recognize your successful vision, goal, gift or talent from the Lord, you must see it as good. You do not need it to be approved by your parents, professor or any other person. You must say it is good and immediately separate it from that which would try to overtake its beauty (the darkness).

To be successful, we must first recognize what we have is beautiful and that it can bring cheerfulness. Afterward, the separation must come, separation is necessary because not everyone is not going to share the same vision of success that

[1] See Strgs#2896

you have for yourself. More often than not, they will not see the same beauty in the light that you see and may even come against it. The separation allows us to see what is for the light and that which is not.

This is where many dreams and visions are crushed. They are crushed because people are searching for validation from friends and family, rather than from God and themselves. When you want to be successful, you must not and cannot look for your approval of success to come from another. You must look upon your vision, goal, and dreams and say they are good. You must protect the light of your vision or idea so that it can eventually birth your success.

> "Imagine opportunities that changes life's limits."
>
> -Dameon Gibbs

After recognizing the good that is in your vision and goal, you must then act on it. And one important way to walk toward it is by simply writing it down. Today's strategist refers to this as a vision board. [Note: maybe put a note in the margin the definition of a vision board]

Habakkuk 2:2 KJV:

2. And the Lord answered me, and said, Write the vision, and make it plain upon tables, that he may run that readeth it.

Many struggle with declaring their vision and goals on earth. They find it hard to complete the very task that the Father has placed in their heart to complete. One reason is that they never start the process, and their dreams and visions are cut short due to fears of failure, or they are too worried about what others may think.

However, the words of the Lord contradict that sort of thinking. He desires for us to overcome fears of failure and fears of what others think. He spoke in **Habakkuk 2:2** as written above, write down the vision (goal) and make it plain.

Before we continue there are a few definitions that I would like to go over.

"Write" is defined as "inscribe, prescribe, subscribe, to engrave, a record."[1] "Vision" is defined as "revelation, dream, a sight."[2] "Plain" is defined as "declare, to explain, to engrave, to dig."[3] "Tables" is defined as "to glisten."[4]

With knowing these definitions, we can then plug them into the verse and get another translation. *"And the Lord answered me, and said, inscribe the dream, and make it declared to glisten."* It is very important that our visions, goals, and ambitions are written down.

By writing them down, you are declaring to the world, to the creation and the universe that your dreams and ambitions are being called forth from your innermost being. What you are thinking on the inside is now being manifested on the outside.

> *You've got to think about big things while you're doing small things, so that all the small things go in the right direction."*
>
> *-Alvin Toffler*

Another interesting term that I want to bring out is "to dig." 'To dig' implies that it is going to take strength to implement your vision. It is a fact that it takes strength and endurance to dig a sizeable hole. We must know that simply because the Lord placed the vision and goal inside us, does not mean that birthing it will be easy. You are going to have to put forth effort, strength, and endurance to see your dream through.

One of the most beautiful aspects of this first principle is the tables. Once your vision is written down upon the tablet it

---

[1] see Strgs#3789
[2] see Strgs#2377
[3] see Strgs#874
[4] see Strgs#3871

16

begins to glisten; remember "tablet" is defined as "to glisten or polish." Writing down your vision makes your vision beautiful to you, as you see what you desire to do or want to accomplish in life. Writing it down is there to encourage you to progress forward. As the scripture suggests, we must run in excitement when reading our goals and ambitions. Seeing the written vision manifest in our life will cause us to shine, meaning what is written will start to reflect on us like a mirror.

The Lord wrote down His vision and it is beautiful. It is so beautiful that there are no other tables like it. From **Genesis 1:1** to **Revelation 22:21** the Lord had written out His vision for His creation. The Bible is His plan and vision for all of creation. How much more should we follow in the Lord's footsteps and write down our visions and goals?

For example, after my wife and I were married, we sat and listed what we wanted to accomplish in the next ten years and listed what we want to accomplish within the next five years of our marriage. And from that moment we immediately began working towards both our long and short-term goals. Over the following years, we frequently referred back to our list to ensure that we were on track. And do you know that within five years we had accomplished both our long and short-term goals? Not because they were easy or that we possessed great skill, it was due to the simple fact that we enjoyed working toward them. As **Habakkuk 2:2** reads, *"that he may run that reads it."* "Run" is defined as to "rush, break down, divide speedily, footman, guard, bring hastily and stretch out."

For our goals, we were happy to be rushing towards that which would bring our family success in the years to come. Breaking down any barriers that attempted to get in our way, while guarding our visions against the wiles of the enemy. It all started with the simple act of writing it down.

For my wife and me it was the simple act of writing out a list of goals. However, for you, the first step of writing it down may mean writing out the overall goal, vision, or ambition that has been placed on your heart and mind. The second step may be to break it down further with charts, calendars, and graphs detailing how you plan to achieve your initial steps, marketing, and networking strategies.

In other words, it is your initial business plan. And the most basic definition of 'business plan' that I found describes it this way. "A business plan is a formal written document containing business goals, the methods on how these goals can be attained, and the time frame that these goals need to be achieved."

We took what the Lord had instructed by writing our goals and visions upon tablets, and applied it to our daily lives. You see the words of the Lord are not only historical and eternal; they are practical.

"Create the highest grandest vision possible for your life, because you become what you believe."

-Oprah Winfrey

Day Two

*"Challenges make you discover things
about yourself that you never really knew,"*

-Cicely Tyson

Day Two
Separate the Vision

Genesis 1:6-8 KJV:

6. And God said, Let there be a firmament in the midst of the waters, and let it divide the waters from the waters.

7. And God made the firmament, and divided the waters which were under the firmament from the waters which were above the firmament: and it was so.

8. And God called the firmament Heaven. And the evening and the morning were the second day.

Here we see God created a need for a division. He divided the Heavens from the earth, and this occurred on Day Two, the day of division. The word divide is the Hebrew word "*badal*" meaning "to separate, distinguish, to differ, and select."[1]

As the Lord was creating the Heavens and the earth, He saw fit to distinguish the two by differing them from one another and separating them using water. How much more should we distinguish our goals and dreams from the world? You have to make your dreams and visions distinguished from the rest.

"If you are working on something exciting that you really care about, you don't have to be pushed. The vision pulls you."

-Steve Jobs

And this is where I believe most Christians and even non-believers, become trapped, as they become discouraged. It is at this very crossroad that many turn back and head back to their

---

[1] see Strgs#914

beginnings, allowing their dreams of success to fade into nothingness. Day Two is a crucial point within the pursuit of success because it is here that one must be willing to divide and separate themselves from others to pursue their visions.

"When you believe in your dream and your vision. Then it begins to attract its own resources. No one was born to be a failure."

-Myles Munroe

As mentioned in Day One, not everyone is going to be on board with your goals and dreams; some may even attempt to sabotage them verbally, emotionally and maybe physically. These are the people or even things that you would need to separate yourself from to help bring your vision to life. It is mentioned in Day One, yet the actual separation occurs on Day Two.

We as Christians must stop holding on to dead weight, while the world is passing us by. If we claim to be of the Most High, our lives should display it, not necessarily with wealth, but by having and displaying a successful lifestyle. By having successful marriages, jobs, family relations, and successful friendships amongst the church body, etc. No matter what angle the world looks at us, they should see success. Why? Because our God is successful and He has ordained us to success as well.

We must learn to separate ourselves from whatever hinders and darkens our ambitions in life. This darkness can take the form of family, friends, coworkers, laziness, or negativity in general. These sorts of elements can stunt the growth of your promise, vision, and goal. Thus they must be cut off and put away with.

Allow me to clarify. I am not referring to separating from responsibilities, such as an ill parent that you are aiding, or something of that nature. For the scripture clearly states, *"honor your mother and father."*[1] "Honor" is defined as "to be made rich or to make glorious."[2]

I am strictly referring to that which is a negative hindrance to you, as its primary goal is to stop you. This is what must be put off. More often than not, moving to new lands means leaving the old behind. And as much as you want and desire, it is impossible to take everyone with you. Sometimes you have to leave others behind to progress. It sounds harsh, but it is the truth. When one goes to college, they do not take their entire community and family. No, they head out alone in hopes to better their lives. There is a natural separation.

"The difference between the impossible and the possible, lies in a person's determination."

-Tommy Lasorda

The majority of us are afraid of the unknown, and this makes us timid when it comes to making a big decision. We are afraid of letting go and moving forward, especially if it is moving on from individuals or things that have somehow been instrumental in our lives. This is when we must remember that people and things can lose their relevance when they no longer line up with what God purposed for our life.

Jesus said it this way in **Matthew 8:22** and **Luke 9:60**, *"Let the dead bury the dead."* In other words, let that which is stagnant and lifeless, commune with that which is stagnant and lifeless. And it is sad to say that we all know and have people and items in our lives that cause us to become stagnant, and do not promote our success. For this cause, the Lord is instructing His people to move on and separate

---

[1] see **Exodus 20:12**
[2] see Strgs#3513

themselves of such dead weight and to be successful and move forward.

This separation may mean staying in and studying while others are out having a fun night out on the town. Or staying up late hours of the night to draw the perfect blueprint for the next technological marvel. In any case, it means going against the norm of what others may be doing. It may even seem bizarre at the time. Yet this is what it takes to birth your vision.

2 Cor. 6:17-18 KJV:

17. Wherefore come out from among them, and be ye separate, saith the Lord, and touch not the unclean thing; and I will receive you.
18. and will be a Father unto you, and ye shall be my sons and daughters, saith the Lord AImighty.

When we receive that grand vision and idea, we must not run and discuss it with everyone that we come across. We must cherish it as though it is treasure because it is. And sometimes the best way to protect an idea or vision is by not sharing it with anyone until the proper time. The body must learn when to be separate, and "separate" in **2 Cor. 6:17** is defined as "to set off by a boundary or limit."

> "Never give up on something that you can't go a day without thinking about."
>
> -Winston Churchill

It is crucial that when we are pursuing our dreams we place limits on negativity. What is important to us should not be caught up in the lifelessness of the world. "Give not that which is holy unto the dogs, neither cast ye your pearls before swine, lest they trample them under their feet, and turn again rend you," KJV.[1] "Rend" is defined as "break, wreck, crack, to sunder, a shattering, disrupt, and lacerate."[2] As a people we must become wise of what we share. What we consider precious can easily be turned to do us harm, whether it be information concerning our family or lyrics to a new worship song. It is important that we take the necessary steps to protect ourselves and visions, even if that means keeping our lips sealed and getting works copy righted, etc.

I remember when I started writing my first book over a decade ago, while I was in college. As soon as I came up with a new idea, theme, setting, or anything remotely related to it, I would run out of my room and run off all the details to my roommates who, at the time, cared little about my writing. And there lay my first mistake.

An Indian proverb states, "Do not reveal what you thought upon doing, but by wise council keep it secret being determined to carry it into execution."

You see, I was too excited about sharing my ideas that it overthrew any logic that I had. Good thing I had great roommates that were completely not interested in novel writing. For I had given them my entire story before it was even copyrighted. In the world that we live in today, it is very easy for ideas and dreams to be stolen, and to be claimed as another original thought. Our vision is our baby and like children we do not hand it over for anyone to watch. Instead, we watch over them and protect them; the same applies to our visions, goals, and ambitions.

The church must be wise, for we receive our counsel from the Lord as we separate unto Him. And He directs us down

---

[1] see **Matthew 7:6**
[2] see Strgs#4486, 2608, 2352 and 3099

the correct paths. My point of saying this, is to say, do not throw your pearls away, have patience, have a plan, have Christ, and separate from dead weight.

If your visions, goals, and aspirations are from the Lord, they are holy. Thus, do not be so quick to toss them to the pigs. Pray to the Father of which routes to take and plan accordingly. The more we separate from the unclean, to join unto the Lord, the more He will relieve us or take favor upon us.

> *"No one has the power to shatter your dreams unless you give it to them."*
>
> *-Maeve Greyson*

Day Three

*"I have not failed, I have just found 10,000
ways that won't work."*

Thomas Edison

Day Three
Give Life to Your Vision

Genesis 1:9-13 KJV:

9. And God said, Let the waters under the heaven be gathered together onto one place, and let the dry land appear: and it was so.

10. And God called the dry land Earth, and the gathering together of the waters called he Seas: and God saw that it was good.

11. And God said, Let the earth bring forth grass, the herb yielding seed, and the fruit tree yielding fruit after his kind, whose seed is in itself, upon the earth: and it was so.

12. And the earth brought forth grass, and herb yielding seed after his kind, and the tree yielding fruit, whose seed was in itself, after his kind: and God saw that it was good.

13. And the evening and the morning were the third day.

Day Three takes the principles of success to a new level. Here we see the introduction of life as God continues to create His marvelous work. Likewise, it is on this day that we must start to produce life concerning our visions, dreams, and ambitions. Day one was the insight and revelation to our vision. Day Two concerned more with separating from that which hinders our vision. As we will read with Day Three, it is here that actual work is needed to bring the revelation of our vision in Day One to life.

> "There are no secrets to success. It is a result of preparation, hard work, and learning from failure."
>
> -Colin Powell

At Day Three, we have reached a point where we start to bring some of the resources that we have collected together similar to how God gathered the waters together into one place in **Genesis 1:9**. These resources should be found in your charts, to-do-lists, calendars, graphs and whatever else you came up with that was initially used in your business plans. The gathering of these resources and information should help give us an idea of where to take and multiply our vision next.

> "Action without vision is only passing time, vision without action is merely day dreaming , but vision with action can change the world."
>
> -Nelson Mandela

The phrase 'gathered together' is the Hebrew word *qavah*, kaw-raw,' meaning "hope, expects to bind together (by twisting), to collect."[1] With Christ as our head, He enables us to find and connect with the correct resources and people, as longs as our intentions are pure. We can bind and twist the resources of the world to our will, gathering them together in a collective location where we can properly utilize them. We must remember that the resources are not going to fall out of the air and onto our lap. Remember, since Day One, we have been planning and collecting data on all topics related to our field, correct? So, when we reach this point, we are ready to begin gathering the resources, and resources bring life to our vision. If the preplanning was never began, one could not pull from an empty storehouse. Now you see why writing down the vision is so important. If the waters (resources) are not gathered, we cannot call forth the life in our vision to grow and multiply.

---

[1] see Strgs#6960

In verse eleven of **Genesis 1**, we read the word yielding twice. I am pointing this out because each of these has a different meaning. The first is the Hebrew word *zara'*, meaning bare, conceive, seed, sower. [1] The second yielding is the Hebrew word *asah*, meaning to make, accomplish, industrious, advance, and to bring forth.[2] If we place these definitions into perspective with our idea of success, we can get a truly eye-opening teaching which is, to bring life to our seed, promise, vision or goal. We must be willing to advance that seed forward.

> *"I had to make my own living and my own opportunity!... Don't sit down and wait for the opportunity to come. You have to get up and make them."*
>
> -Madam C.J. Walker

This means that we cannot get stuck at Day One and Two, the church can no longer start something and not finish it. I cannot count how much talent I have seen wasted over the years, as people continue to use the same excuses: "I don't have time," "I started, and I plan to get back to it," "I don't have the money," "it's too late now." These are all lazy excuses, excuses the enemy encourages us to continue using. Why, because they do not want us to achieve the greatness that the Lord promised us. Excuses are merely a hindrance to keep us from achieving our vision which is our God-given talent.

When we wake up in the morning our minds should be focused on three things:

❖ How can I do the work of the Lord?
❖ How can I build up my family?

---

[1] see Strgs#2232
[2] see Strgs#6213

❖ What do I need to do to make progress toward my vision?

I like the definition "industrious" for "yield". We must become more industrious when bringing our vision to life. Webster's Dictionary defines "industrious" as "hardworking, tireless, characterized by hard work and perseverance." The Body of Christ must put forth hard work and persevere through all tribulations. The body must put forth perseverance if it desires to see its visions and promises fulfilled. Visions are not fulfilled without effort.

"Effort" is simply defined as an 'earnest and conscientious activity intended to do or accomplish something.' Effort could be spending more time doing or with that particular thing, drawing up more drafts, more study, handing out flyers, sending out more query letters after being rejected fifty times already or finalizing that recipe. Effort is being industrious and industrious is making the necessary sacrifices to see your vision come to life.

> "Never limit your vision based on your current resources."
>
> -Michael Hyatt

We must realize the God-given authority in us and declare to ourselves and the world, that we will succeed. No more failing, for it is time to birth what is in us, bringing forth the seed. God spoke to the waters to gather, He called dry land to appear and commanded the plants to bear fruit. How much more should we follow suit? Yes, we are not God, nor should we attempt to be. Yet God gave humanity dominion over the earth and the resources thereof.[1] When resources are running low, or things

------

[1] see **Genesis 1:28**

seems like they are no longer falling into place for you, speak and declare to your resources to be released and collected into one place to be used.

Through **Genesis 1:9-13** the scripture reads God <u>said</u> verse nine and <u>called</u> verse ten. "Said" once again is the Hebrew word "*amar*," <u>aw-mar'</u>, meaning "to speak to say, answer, appoint, certify, challenge and command."[1] "Called" is the Hebrew word "*qara*," <u>kaw-raw</u>, which is defined as "to address by name, cry, invite, proclaim, publish, read, and bidden."[2]

From the Hebrew definitions, we can gather that when God was calling this world into existence, He was doing it with a purpose, vision, and with authority. He challenged and appointed the waters as seen in verse nine, and called out the earth by name with a cry as He published it. The resources of this world bowed and obeyed His every command.

Galatian 4:6 KJV:

6. And because ye are sons, God hath sent forth the spirit of his son into your hearts, crying, Abba, father.

1 Peter 2:9 KJV:

9. But ye are a chosen generation, a royal priesthood, an holy nation, a peculiar people; that ye should shew forth the praises of him who hath called you out of darkness into his marvelous light.

Matthew 21:18-21 KJV:

---

[1] see Strgs#559
[2] see Strgs#7121

18. Now in the morning as he returned into the city, he hungered.

19. And when he saw a fig tree in the way, he came to it, and found nothing thereon, but leaves only, and said unto it, let no fruit grow on thee henceforward for ever. And presently the fig tree withered away.

> "Success seems to be largely a matter of hanging on after others have let go."
>
> -William Feather

20. And when the disciples saw it, they marveled, saying, How soon is the fig tree withered away!

21. Jesus answered and said unto them, verily I say unto you, if ye have faith, and doubt not, ye shall not only do this which is done to the fig tree, but also if ye shall say unto this mountain, Be thou removed, and be thou cast into the sea; it shall be done.

Proverbs 18:21 KJV:

21. Death and life are in the power of the tongue: and they that love it shall eat the fruit thereof.

I went through these four passages to bring out the correlation of speaking and declaring. All believers that call on the name of Jesus are saved and being saved we become sons, and, daughters, and part of the holy priesthood. Being sons and daughters, Christ Himself said that we should be able to call out to the resources of the earth to come to our aid. We are royalty, and when we enter or exit an arena, we must be treated as such.

The resources of this planet are at your disposal for Godly purposes. So speak to your environment that it may produce fruit for your journey in life. Then use those resources to work hard and bring forth the promised seed of the vision inside of you. Do not draw back when complications come your way or when resources seem to be dissipating. But take up your Godly position and call out to what you need by name and appoint it to where it is needed. It's time that we put boots on the ground and begin working to bring our visions to life. Remember death, life, power, authority, and direction lay within the very words that we speak.

Day Four

"The world of great opportunity is available now, as it has always been, only for those with great vision."

-Andrew Carnegie

Day Four
Steer Your Vision

Genesis 1:14-19 KJV:

14. And God said, let there be lights in the Firmament of the heaven to divide the day from the night, and let them be for signs, and for seasons, and for days, and for years:

15. And let them be for lights in the firmaments of the heaven to give light upon the earth: and it was so.

16. And God made two great lights; the greater light to rule the day, and the lesser light to rule the night: he made the stars also.

17. And God set them in the firmament of the heaven to give light upon the earth,

18. And to rule over the day and over the night, and to divide the light from the darkness: and God saw that it was good.[1]

19. And the evening and the morning were the forth day.

"Leadership is the capacity to translate vision into reality."

-Warren Bennis

Here in creation day four, God created the Sun, Moon, and Stars. And according to **Genesis 1:14** their sole purpose was to divide day and night through rulership. God made two great lights, one to rule the day and the other to rule the night. "Rule" in verse sixteen is defined as "rule, ruler,

---

[1] good = Hebrew *tob*, tobe, meaning beautiful, cheerful, loving pleasure, wealth [Strgs#2896]

dominion, reign, or exercise dominion."[1] Webster's defines "exercise" as "a task performed, or problem solved in order to develop skill or understanding."

Now, let us put this information into perspective to make sense of it. The purpose of Day Four is to help reveal the importance of understanding rulership and leadership. Day Four is all about taking leadership over our visions, goals, and ambitions. Doing all that we need to do, to develop the necessary skills to perform the task that was put forth in Day Three, no longer waiting for the help and report of others to guide us.

"A genuine leader is not a searcher for consensus, but a molder of consensus."

-Martin Luther King, Jr.

On Day Four we see the building of self-assurance, where we are relying on ourselves to see task performed, not others. Not saying having others perform a task for us is wrong, by no means is that the message, as some tasks cannot be completed without the help of others. However, the message is that we are the ruler and leader of the vision that has been set forth. As more people become involved there is a greater chance of influences being placed upon your established vision. This is where the leader needs to step up and keep the vision in place that things do not go astray. A leader not only protects the vision, but he or she also knows which directions to take the vision in.

By Day Four we should no longer be stumbling and wandering around the wilderness with our vision. Our minds should be made up, and we should be in route to the Promised Land.

_____

[1] see Strgs#4475]

Numbers 13:26-33 KJV:

26. And they went and came to Moses, and to Aaron, and to all the congregation of the children of Israel, on to the wilderness of Paran, to Kadesh; and brought back word unto them, and unto all the congregation, and shewed them the fruit of the land.

> "It's not that I'm smart. It's just that I stay with problems longer."
>
> -Albert Einstein

27. And they told him, and said, We came unto the land whither thou sentest us, and surely it floweth with milk and honey, and this is the fruit of it.

28. Nevertheless the people be strong that dwell in the land, and the cities are walled, and very great: and moreover, we saw the children of Anak there.

29. The Amalekites dwell in the land of the south: and the Hittites, and the Jebusites, and the Amorites, dwell in the mountains: and Canaanites dwell by the sea, and by the coast of Jordan.

30. And Caleb stilled the people before Moses, and said, Let us go up at once, and possess it, for we are well able to overcome it.

31. But the men that went up with him said, We be not able to go up against the people; for they are stronger than we.

32. And they brought up an evil report of the land which they had searched unto the children of Israel, saying, The land, through which we have gone to search it, is a land that eateth up the inhabitants thereof, and all the people that we saw in it are men of a great stature.

33. And there we saw the giants, the Sons of Anak, which come of the giants: and we were in our own sight as grasshoppers, and so we were in their sight.

Just as God declares words over us, He did the same for the children of Israelites. He promised them a land flowing with milk and honey, and He kept His word and delivered that to them. They saw the bountifulness of the land with their eyes, yet they immediately became discouraged when they noticed they had to fight to obtain their promise. And instead of fighting, they begin to make excuses of why they could not obtain the Promise Land, a land that God had already said was theirs.

Now we must ask ourselves, how many of us have reached pivotal points in our lives where we were destined to accomplish something? When we fold under the prospect of a fight; then we make excuses of why we gave up. We make it right to the point where we are almost over the hill but when the giants come, we falter, not realizing that our God is bigger than any situation or excuse.

> *"Our greatest glory is not in never falling but in rising every time we fall."*
>
> *-Confucius*

We cannot afford to be like the children of Israel and see what the Promise Land has to offer yet be too afraid to take it. If anything, when we see the land and all the milk and honey that flows in it, that should energize us to push forward more. God's word in our life, should be a motivating factor, not a deterrent. His word should drive us to Him. It should drive us to His son; it should drive us toward our vision.

Far too long has the church sat by and made excuses about the giants in their lives. Now it is about time that we step up and address the true issues that have hindered so many of God's people from seeking out their vision and goals. And once again it is fear.

What was the second thing the spies reported back to Moses when they returned? *"Nevertheless the people be strong that dwell in the land and the cities are walled and very great.*

42

And moreover, we saw the children of Anak there."[1] Their very words were meant to drive a wedge of fear into the hearts of the congregation. Their words were so dishearting that Caleb had to get the people to hold their tongue. Verse thirty-two goes as far to call their words an <u>evil report</u> of the land. An evil report is defined as "slander or defaming."[2]

Fear wants to defame us; it wants to defame the divine promise of God in us. Fear does not want us to succeed in anything. Thus it will throw whatever it can at us, to get us off track. It wants us to focus on the smaller issue of giants and not the larger picture of success. We must make our vision larger than the giants/excuses/fears instead of them being larger than our vision. More importantly, we cannot take on the fear of others as our own. As we will come to see, Joshua and Caleb did not share the same fears as those giving the report. Likewise, we cannot take on the fears of our parents, siblings, friends, and coworkers. We must experience the land for ourselves, as their experience must not become your experience.

> "Leadership is about vision and responsibility, not power."
>
> -Seth Berkley

Knowing this we have to be cautious and aware of not projecting our fears onto others, especially onto children. For it is easy to project our fears onto the developing minds and then label it as simply being a concern. It is important that our reports are true, realistic, laying out the fight ahead, yet making the end goal the focal point.

---

[1] see **Numbers 13:28**
[2] see Strgs#1681

Reaching success is much larger than all the little things that attempt to hinder us from reaching success. Because of their fears, these people held themselves back from being leaders of their visions and ambitions. Let's continue reading to see how true leaders react in such situations.

Numbers 14:1-10 KJV:

1. And all the congregation lifted up their voice, and cried, and the people wept that night.
2. And all the children of Israel murmured against Moses and against Aaron: and the whole congregation said unto them, would God that we had died in the land of Egypt! or would God we had died in this wilderness.
3. And wherefore hath the Lord brought us into this land, to fall by the sword, that our wives and our children should be a prey? were it not better for us to return into Egypt?
4. And they said one to another, let us make a captain, and let us return into Egypt.
5. Then Moses and Aaron fell on their faces before all the assembly of the congregation of the children of Israel.
6. And Joshua the son of Nun, and Caleb, the son of Jephunneh, which were of them that search the land, rent their clothes.
7. And they spake unto all the company of the children of Israel, saying, The lands which we passed through to search it, is an exceeding good land.
8. If the Lord delight in us, then he will bring us into this land, and give it us; a land which floweth with milk and honey.
9. Only rebel not ye against the Lord, neither fear ye the people of the land; for they are bread for us: their defense is departed from them, and the Lord is with us: Fear them not.

10. But all the congregation bade stone them with stones. And the glory of the Lord appeared in the tabernacle of the congregation before all the children of Israel.

What makes us leaders of our dreams, goals, and ambitions, is how we react when the world comes against them. We see something positive beyond the horizon, yet those around us only see the negative. It is here that a leader must take a stand for what he or she wants. Let us take a closer look at the actions of Joshua and Caleb, to see how they reacted when those they cared for came against their promise.

Numbers 14 is a continuation of chapter 13, where the spies are giving their report to Moses and Aaron. And their words caused the congregation of Israel to murmur. The evil and fearful report that they brought back to the camp began to affect the camp negatively. Fear is contagious. Fear is a stumbling block against one's dreams and ambitions.

"Murmured" in **Numbers 14:2** is defined as "to pass the night, to be obstinate, complaint, lie all night, lodge, and tarry."[1] I like to define "murmur" as "being lazy and to pass over the promise." These individuals were so stuck on the past and fearful of what the future could hold for them that they were willing to go back into the bondage of Egypt or back into a familiar place instead of progressing.

> And let us not be weary in well doing: for in due season we shall reap, if we faint not.
>
> -Galatians 9:6

---

[1] see Strgs#3885

The people of Israel looked to their past to find reasons why they could not be successful. So likewise, many of us do the same, digging into our past to find reasons why we cannot be successful: I am too old, my credit is bad, my parents always said I would be nothing, I never finished high school, etc. These are all lies and murmurs of the enemy to get us off focus from the promise of success. They completely ignored the promises of the Lord, although the proof of the promise lay before their eyes. They would rather sit around and conjure up excuses of why they cannot, instead of why they can.

> "Optimism is the faith that leads to achievement. Nothing can be done without hope and confidence."
>
> -Helen Keller

If we plan to be successful, we must find a reason, to achieve our promise and stop being lazy murmurers. We must stop passing the night away with unproductivity, for our promise will not be achieved if we never walk towards it due to fear. Being the leaders of our vision, we must be like Joshua and Caleb, and combat lies and murmuring with the truth of what God has spoken over us. For the Lord is righteous and will see us through to the end.

They spoke according to what the Lord said and by what they saw. Verse six stated that Joshua and Caleb were with the spies when they searched the land. "Searched" is defined as "to meander, to seek, merchant, and be excellent." Being with the spies they saw the same things. Although they saw the same, their reports are very different.

Joshua and Caleb knew how to navigate and meander their way in the Promised Land. They went into the Promised Land seeking the milk and honey that was promised to them by the Lord. They were like merchants ready to make use of the new found resources. I am certain that they did not enter the Promised Land and say to themselves "I'm sure none of what God said is here." No, that would be foolish. I am sure they entered the land and saw the same giants, how could they not? However, I am certain they had a mindset that was more interested and focused on seeing a land flowing with milk and honey than worrying about the problems of the land. A land that the Lord had been guiding them towards for years. Why would their minds be on anything else; they were anticipating the Promise Land. They went in expecting what was spoken over them. Their vision, anticipation, and expectations outweighed any fears.

We must search out the ways of success. Listen to others report of how they achieve success. We must search out the ways of a merchant and come up with our positive report of the land, stating that our promise will flow with milk and honey. For the land is lush with grapes, pomegranates, and figs. In doing so, we must become vigilant of those that desire to stone/kill our vision and dreams. As these can be those within our congregation (friends and family), as "company" in verse seven translates as "family, crowd, assembly, and people." It is here that we learn and trust in the words of the Lord that He has spoken to us through His prophets or Holy Spirit. His promise is a protection for us, and it cannot be broken, for He is a God that cannot break His promises. **Titus 1:2** reads, *"In hope of eternal life, which God, that cannot lie, promise before the world began."* Knowing this we must become like Joshua and Caleb concerning the promise.

Joshua and Caleb were the two that took charge of their promise of success when others fell back in fear. As the old saying goes, we must "grab the bull by the horn," even if it means getting knocked down. Do you know that many of the world's wealthiest families remain that way by passing the knowledge of how to run a business successfully down to the next generation? Are we passing on the knowledge to the next generation of how to be successful? Are we conquering fears so that they do not pass on to the next generation? If we exterminate the giants in our lifetime, how can they become

47

fears of next generation if they no longer exist? Become a leader of your vision, end the murmuring (laziness), defeat the giants (fear), and search out the land for resources.

Once in the Promised Land we must know how to search and utilize the resources that are at our disposal, always remembering that nothing is too large or small for our vision.

There are two additional points I would like to discuss before closing this chapter. First, in **Genesis 2:15**, it states, *"And the Lord took the man, and put him into the garden of Eden to dress it and to Keep it."* Secondly, **Numbers 14:6-8**, stated when Joshua and Caleb gave their report of the Promised Land, they reported of an exceeding good land, a land flowing with milk and honey.

> *"However difficult life may seem, there is always something you can do, and succeed at. It matters that you don't just give up."*
>
> -Stephen Hawking

Whenever God promises us or places us in an environment, the particular environment in which He settles us, will have all the resources we need to thrive. In **Genesis 2:15**, God put Adam in the Garden of Eden, a place of pleasure, for Eden literally translate as *pleasure* in Hebrew. It was there in which God instructed Adam to dress and keep the garden. Adam was made responsible for using the Eden's resources, although having no prior knowledge on how to do so. We also read in **Numbers 14** of how God gave the Israelites a land flowing with milk and honey, yet the Israelites were responsible for driving out the current inhabitants of land if they wish to possess the land.

Do you see it? Do you understand? God sometimes places us in environments which has all the necessary resources we need to thrive, yet we are made responsible for capturing, dressing, and keeping the resources of the land. Dress in **Genesis 2:15** is the Hebrew word *'âbad*, <u>aw-bad'</u>, meaning to work, to serve, till, enslave.[1] 'Âbad consist of the Hebrew pictographs, *ayin, bet,* and *dalet. Ayin* (literally picture of an eye) means to see, know, and experience. *Bet* (literally picture of a house) means household, in into, and family. *Dalet* (literally a picture of a door) means pathway and to enter. Therefore, if we were to read *'âbad* pictographically, it could read as the following, to experience the household by entering the door.

It is our duty or we are charge with experiencing the things within the house (environment/place of dwelling) and we do this simply by entering through the door[2] of opportunity. And though we may not know how to gather and use the resources initially, we must over time train ourselves and learn how to. We cannot afford to complain about the giants or snakes wandering about in our Promise Land. If anything, we must crush and overcome any obstacles present.

Keep in **Genesis 2:15** comes from the Hebrew word *shâmar,* meaning to guard, to protect, attend, to hedge about with thorns.[3] *Shâmar* consist of the Hebrew letters *sheen, mem,* and *reysh. Sheen,* which is the picture of tooth, means to consume or to destroy. *Mem* is pictured by water, meaning chaos. Then there is *reysh* which is the picture of a person or head. Reading *Shâmar* as a picture word could read as, to destroy the chaotic person or to destroy the chaotic head.

Who is the chaotic head that came to roam in the garden, that would be the serpent?[4] And we are responsible for crushing the head of any obstacle/serpent which attempts to prevent us from using our God-given resources.[5]

---

[1] see Strgs#5647

[2] compare **John 10:7-9**

[3] see Strgs#8104

[4] see **Genesis 3:1**

[5] compare **Genesis 3:15** & **Luke 10:19**

Day Five

"There are seven days in the week and someday isn't one of them."

-Dr. O'Neal

Day Five
Increase Your Productivity

Genesis 1:20-23 KJV:

20. And God said, Let the waters bring forth abundantly the moving creatures that hath life, and fowl that may fly above the earth in the open firmament of heaven.

21. And God created great whales and every living creature that moveth, which the waters brought for the abundantly, after their kind, and every winged fowl after his kind: God saw that it was good.

22. And God blessed them, saying, Be fruitful, and multiply, and fill the waters in the seas, and let fowl multiply in the earth.

23. And the evening and the morning were the fifth day.

Day Five is all about multiplying, increasing productivity, increasing steps, and progressing even further. Reaching this day is a great milestone as it is a point where we can begin to reproduce and multiply what we have already sown. This increase in productivity will vary from vision to vision. For some, an increase with productivity may be more dedicated time to write because they are an author and for another, it may be hiring more people to keep up with the demand of a product. If one desires to see the success of their marriage, time, productivity, and activity are needed. And hopefully, by this point in our vision, we will know which areas to focus on and be more productive in.

> *"Opportunities multiply as they are seized."*
>
> *-Sun Tzu*

Increase and productivity are the focus of Day Five as seen in the few keywords mentioned in **Genesis 1:20-23**. Those words and phrases are 'bring forth abundantly,' 'be fruitful, and 'multiply.' "Bring forth abundantly" is the Hebrew *sharats*, shaw-rats, meaning to "swarm, to teem, to wriggle, abound, increase, in abundance and move."[1] "Be fruitful" is the Hebrew word *parah*, paw-rah, which is defined as "to bear fruit, branch off, to show fruitfulness, grow and increase."[2] And is last is "multiply" which is the Hebrew word *rabab*, raw-bab, meaning "to become great, to increase, be in authority, excel, bring up, abundance."[3]

Reading this may have you reflecting on Day Three which focused on giving and speaking life to your vision. As seen in the definitions above, Day Five has an entirely different focus, yet connects to life. With Day Five, we want our vision to be abounding, increasing, and swarming forward like insects. Our vision should be taking on new grounds as it begins to branch off, bringing life to other areas of our life, not just the area we originally intended. Last, our vision causes us to become great and teaches us how to excel. Not saying that everyone will become president or become a millionaire, but that in our eyes and those around us, we will be seen as great, becoming great teachers, parents, husband and wives, friends, lawyers or athletes will ultimately bring great esteem to us and even those around us.

> "You multiply your time by spending time on things today that will give you more time tomorrow."
>
> -Roy Vaden

[1] see Strgs#8317
[2] see Strgs#6509
[3] see Strgs#7232

Now let me tackle the beast that is the topic of living paycheck to pay check; which many of us do. And yes, I do believe it to be a hindrance to God's people, unless He deemed it for His will. Otherwise, God's people are meant to multiply their talents and a cycle such as this keeps us from multiplying and birthing. It keeps us focused on how much money we made, how much money will be left over after the bills are paid, and will there be enough to sustain us to our next pay? This is a stressful state to constantly live in; it is a state that the enemy wants us to remain in. Because the longer we remain in such a state, the less we focus on bettering our future.

> *"The best preparation for tomorrow is doing your best today."*
>
> -H. Jackson Brown, Jr.

In **Matthew 25:14-30** we read of the master who gave his servants talents. "Talent" is the Greek word *talanton*, tal-an-ton; meaning a "balance, weight, coin or sum of money."[1] The principle that I want to bring from this is the fact that the Lord has given us all a talent in life (a skill to do a job).

As witnessed in this passage it is our duty to multiply that talent, both physically and spiritually. In essence, living paycheck to paycheck I see as being both a means of spiritual and physical bondage. Why, because it hinders us from multiplying the talent the Lord provided us. The thought of not having money binds us mentally and spiritually, while not actually having money is the physical bondage. Yet we must break this curse and act of bondage. And we break it by preparing for the future.

When I say preparing, I mean storing a few dollars aside from each check to pay for school, or a heat press to make t-

---

[1] See Strgs#5007

shirts or whatever we are saving toward. This would be taking a step to multiplying your talents and not settling on our one talent. I am not stating that if you are in a situation where you are living pay check to paycheck that it is a sin, I am simply giving the principle of how to possibly multiply your talent to end that situation. As we are not made to live in a constant financial struggle, there may be some struggle but not a lasting one. So even in your current financial state, think and pray of how you can multiply the talents you possess for your future circumstances. If you are not in this financial battle the same can apply, store up and prepare for your future.

God wants us to grow and multiply. He never intended for us to be a stagnant species. He never wanted us to be stagnant in our relationship with Him or within our daily lives. It is all about increase, growth, mobility, and productivity. How can anyone ever expect to become a better individual if there is no growth on the inside or out? Being productive causes your vision to grow and multiply. And the fruits of that growth will be more growth. Meaning, the more we produce and grow, the more other people will want to produce and grow. A byproduct of one person's success is hope for another.

> "Success is not the key to happiness. Happiness is the key to success. If you love what you are doing, you will be successful."
>
> -Albert Schweitzer

Verse twenty-one clearly states that the creatures would multiple and bring forth after their kind. I take this as being two-fold, the first being, that as we increase in our vision that whatever our vision entails it will increase. Secondly, as we increase and multiply that we will produce more individuals like ourselves. These are people that desire to make something of themselves. People that want Christ to reveal their vision for their life and household, and they will come to you seeking counsel. This is the reason why individuals chase after celebrities they desire fame, fashion and glory yet have not achieved it for themselves. They lack the vision and ambition of their own, so they blindly follow another's. Well, it is about time that we tell people that the success of their vision does not lay in another human being but with God. For God is the only one that can reveal your vision, purpose, and then place you the road to success.

Now go and multiple your vision and dreams. Nothing can stop you from succeeding except you. And being the entrepreneur that you are, do not be afraid to train another individual up on the steps of success. You never know, your words could change their life.

Day Six

"Some people dream of success, while other people get up every morning and make it happen."

-Wayne Huizenga

Day Six
Taking Up Dominion

Genesis 1:24-31 KJV:

24. And God said, Let the earth bring forth the living creature after his kind, cattle after his kind, cattle, and creeping thing, and beast of the earth after his kind: and it was so.

25. And God made the beast of the earth after his kind, and cattle after their kind, and everything that creepeth upon the earth after his kind: and God saw that it was good.

26. And God said, Let us make man in our image, after our likeness; and let them have dominion over the fish of the sea, and over the fowl of the air, and over the cattle, and over all the earth and over every creeping thing that creepeth upon the earth.

27. So God created man in his own image, in the image of God created he him; male and female created he them.

28. And Got blessed them, and God said unto them, Be fruitful, and multiply, and replenish the earth, and subdue it: and have dominion over the fish of the sea, and over the fowl of the sea, and over the fowl of the air, and over every living thing that moveth upon the earth.

29. And God said, Behold, I have given you every herb bearing seed, which is upon the face of all the earth, and every tree, in the which is the fruit of a tree yielding seed; to you, it shall be for meat.

30. And to every beast of the earth, and to every fowl of the air, and to every thing that creepeth upon the earth, wherein there is life, I have given every green herb for meat: and it was so.

31. And God saw everything that he had made, and behold; it was very good. And the evening and the morning were the sixth day.

Like Day Five there is some multiplication that takes place. Yet this is not the standout difference. Unlike Day Five, in Day Six we must take up our position of dominion when it comes to our vision. For it is a position that was purposed to us by God. With this position, He has given us the ability to rule over the necessary resources. As "dominion" in verse twenty-eight is defined as "to tread down, subjugate, crumble off, prevail against and reign."[1] He not only called us to dominate but also to subdue. "Subdue" is the Hebrew word *kabash*, <u>kaw-bash</u>, which is defined as "to tread down, to disregard, to conquer, and bring to bondage."[2] Not only are we supposed to prevail when it comes to our vision, but we must also tread down and conquer as well. What makes Day Six even more important is the fact, that it is the only day that God considered very good. Days one through five God referred to them as being good, yet when He finished day six, He called it very good.

> *"The secret of change is to focus all of your energy, not on fighting the old, but on building the new."*
>
> *-Socrates*

A day that man was created on and the day that He commanded our dominion. "Very" is simply defined as "exceedingly, might, force and abundance."[3] Keep in mind that "good" is defined as "beautiful, cheerful, graciously, pleasure and precious."[4] So in God's eyes, us having dominion over our vision is exceedingly pleasureful to Him. Why you may ask, because He never intended for our life to be chaotic. He wants us to take charge and dominate all aspects of our

---

[1] see Strgs#7287
[2] see Strgs#3533
[3] see Strgs#3966
[4] see Strgs#2896

life, with Him as our head. He wants us to take charge of our families, our marriages, our ambitions and positions within the body.

The question remains, how do we apply the concepts of dominion, subjugation and conquering to our visions. We apply it to our life through the idea of knowledge. We conquer our vision by knowing all we can regarding it. To be dominant, we must know our field of work. If you have been working toward opening your business, you need to have the necessary knowledge to do so. That means reading the necessary books, watching the necessary videos, attending workshops, and talking to the proper people, doing all to become an expert. This applies to those whose vision is to better relationships or running for a city office.

> "Each day is a new opportunity. I chose to make this day a great one."
>
> -Louise L. Hay

Ephesians 6:11 reads, *"Put on the whole armor of God, that you may be able to stand against the wiles of the devil."* "Put on" comes from the Greek word *enduo*, en-doo'-o, meaning "array, to invest with clothing."[1] Paul was informing the Ephesians to wear the armor of God because it allowed them to combat the wiles of the devil.

Now to completely understand what Paul was getting at here, we must come to understand something about the Ephesians or the ancient world. To refer to anything soldier related would be the equivalent of referring to the American police officer. Talking about ancient soldiers' armor pieces would be the same as pointing out a police firearm. Seeing

---

[1] see Strgs#1746

63

soldiers in town was normal for the Ephesians and was perfect for Paul to draw from.

Paul knew that the Ephesians understood how armor worked and how it protected the body, making the analogy of God's armor easier to understand. What I want to bring out is the idea that one cannot simply put on the armor and expect to be efficient in it. Unlike us, the Ephesians saw soldiers on a regular basis and knew that the soldiers wore the armor daily, they trained in it, they marched in it. In other words, the soldiers took on all the necessary training to become more efficient in the armor so that in time of war it would not hinder their ability to fight. Equate this to a basketball player stepping onto the court to play but yet never picked up a basketball one day in their life.

> *"Strength and growth come only through continuous effort and struggle."*
>
> *-Napoleon Hill*

We can <u>stand against</u> the devil because we properly trained in the armor of God. As believers, we should all be wearing the girt of truth, the breastplate of righteousness, boots of the gospel of peace, and shield of faith.[1] "Stand against"[2] means "to continue forward" and we continue forward by having trained up in the armor.

That was the spiritual side of **Eph. 6:11**, the practical truth remains the same. To defeat and conquer our visions and goals, we must become masters of the armor. We must be willing to stand against the opposition based on the knowledge, training, and faith we have acquired. Without

------

[1] see **Eph. 6:14-16**

[2] stand against comes from two Greek words, *histemi* for stand meaning abide, appoint, continue, covenant [see Strgs#2476]. And *pros* for against, meaning forward, toward [see Strgs#4314].

them, we would be nothing more than a soldier on a battlefield that has never mastered their equipment.

By having strong knowledge and training of our goals, it keeps us from being led astray from our vision. It takes strength to stay on course with the vision and knowledge of the vision enables the dominion to be released. Let us read Matthew for example.

Matthew 4:1-11 KJV:

1. Then was Jesus led up of the spirit into the wilderness to be tempted of the devil.
2. And when he had fasted forty days and forty nights, he was afterward an hungered.
3. And when the tempter came to him, he said, If thou be the Son of God, command that these stones be made bread.
4. But he answered and said, It is written, Man shall not live by bread alone, but by every word that proceedeth out of the mouth of God.
5. Then the devil taketh him up into the holy city, and setteth him on a pinnacle of the temple,
6. And saith on to him, If thou be the Son of God, cast thyself down; for it is written, He shall give his angels charge concerning thee: and in their hands, they shall bear thee up, Lest at any time thou dash thy foot against a stone.
7. Jesus said unto him, It is written again, Thou shalt not tempt the Lord thy God.
8. Again, the devil taketh him up into an exceeding high mountain, and sheweth him all the kingdoms of the world, and the glory of them;
9. And saith unto him, All these things will I give thee, if thou wilt fall down and worship me.

10. Then saith Jesus onto him, Get thee hence, Satan: for it is written, Thou shalt worship the Lord thy God, and him only shalt thou serve.

11. Then the devil leaveth him, and behold, angels came and ministered unto him.

Even Christ understood the dominion that came with Knowledge, and He demonstrated it for our benefit. Being Lord and Savior, He could have called upon His angels as the devil suggested. But all that was not necessary, for the dominion to stand against the devil was in His knowledge. Jesus simply referenced His knowledge of the scripture to withstand the devil. He did not call the devil out of his name, accuse him of anything or degrade him. He simply used His knowledge by saying, "It is written."

> "We must keep moving. Do not sit down. Do not say 'I have done enough.' Always see what else you can do to raise Hell with the enemy. You must have a desperate determination to continually go forward."
>
> -General George S. Patton Jr.

Jesus saw God's vision and plan for His life, and so prepared himself accordingly. With His Father as His head, He wielded dominion and power as a true leader, not allowing anything to hinder Him from that vision. The power of knowledge can be the difference between success and failure. Its up to us to obtain the necessary knowledge to see our vision through to the end.

2 Timothy 2:15 states, *"Study to show yourself approved unto God."* The word "study" comes from a Greek word meaning "to use speed, be prompt, give diligence and labor."[1]

---

[1] see Strgs#4704

"Approved" is defined as "acceptable."[1] In other words, we should constantly be diligently working to improve our knowledge before God. And not just of Him but of all that He desires for us to accomplish. This could be people to meet, places to visit, or things to do; all of which require some level of knowledge and knowledge equals dominion.

> "The wall! Your success is on the other side. Can't jump over it or go around it. You know what to do."
>
> -Dwayne 'The Rock' Johnson

---

[1] see Strgs#1384

Day Seven

"Rest is not idleness, and to lie sometime, on the grass under trees on a summer's day, listening to the murmur of the water, or watching the clouds float across the sky, is by no means a waste of time."

-John Lubbock

Day Seven
Rest In Your Vision

Genesis 2:1-3 KJV:

1. Thus the heavens and the earth were finished, and all the host of them.
2. And on the seventh day God ended his work which he had made; and he rested on the seventh day from all his work which he had made.
3. And God blessed the seventh day, and sanctified it: because that in it he had rested from all his work which God created and made.

This is the day that we all strive for when it comes to success. Day Seven is the day of rest. It is the day that we look back at and smile at our success. And just as the Lord rested on the Seventh Day, we must learn to rest in the success of the vision we had set out to create since Day One. It is about resting in our work, promise, and vision with a complete sense of accomplishment and happiness.

> "Good, better, best. Never let it rest. 'Til your good is better and better is best."
>
> -St. Jerome

To understand Day Seven let us first define a few words that will be referred to frequently throughout this chapter. Those words are:

* finished - *kalah*, <u>kaw-law</u> = to end, to cease, consume, determine.[1]

---

[1] see Strgs#3615

- ❖ work - *melakah,* <u>mel-aw-kaw</u> = deputy ship, ministry, employment, business, labor, industrious, and occupation.[1]
- ❖ made - *asah,* <u>aw-saw</u> = accomplish, advance, appoint, work, produce.[2]
- ❖ rested - *shabath,* <u>shaw-bath</u> = to repose, desist, exertion, cease and celebrate.[3]

In light of these definitions, let us revisit and insert a couple of them into the previous passage.

Genesis 2:1-3 KJV:

1. Thus the heavens and the earth were <u>determined</u>, and all the host of them.
2. And on the seventh day God ended his <u>business</u> which he had <u>produce</u>, and he <u>celebrated</u> on the seventh day from all his <u>labor</u> which he had appointed.
3. And God blessed the seventh day, and sanctified it: because that in it he had <u>exerted</u> from all his <u>business</u> which God created and <u>accomplished</u>.

The Lord celebrated on the seventh day of His labor, yet He had exerted Himself completely into His business. Yes, we know the Lord is all powerful and can do all. Thus He cannot truly exert Himself as in exhaust, but that He put to use the resources before Him. The idea that we must take from this is that He had given all to His creation—He has given all to it because in His eyes He saw it as being good. And once He had determined that the business He had produce was finished,

---

[1] see Strgs#4399
[2] see Strgs#6213
[3] see Strgs#7673

He celebrated its completion and rested in it. The resources and effort He put into His work was worth it in His eyes; it had value and purpose.

Knowing the efforts the Lord placed into His business and seeing His accomplishments, how much more should we work toward the same determination, reaching the day that we come to celebrate our accomplishments? In Days even we should be happy to see our vision being fulfilled, as happiness is a sign to us that our vision is being fulfilled. When we rest in our vision, we should wake up happy, looking forward to what the day brings. This means that we had given everything that we have into the business, into the ministry, into the goal, into the vision, into the labor. Day Seven is seeing the fruit and accumulation of all our labors breaking forth: the vision, separation, giving life, being a leader, increasing productivity, and taking dominion. If anything, it is when we are not working within our visions that causes us to be discouraged and unhappy. And many people fall victim to this because they do not see the work that they are producing as being good.

> "If you want to be successful in this world, you have to follow your passion, not a paycheck."
>
> -Jen Welter

For example, most people in America work for other people, and by working for that person or company, they are paid their wages. Well by working for another person they are ultimately working to see the company's goals met, not their own. And all they get out of it is a check and maybe insurance. So, if you truly look at it, by working for another, we are not producing for ourselves and inwardly may not see it as being good. We need to be producing something in our lives for ourselves so that we can say it is good.

I was once in this situation, where I was working the regular nine to five job. Yes, it paid the necessary family bills, but on the inside, I was not happy. Every day I dreaded going into work, and I am not saying that my job was horrible by any means. The fact was that my job was not leading me towards any of my life's visions or goals. Eventually, I had to make a choice, leave the job that paid well and took care of all my bills, yet left me unfulfilled. Or leave it to pursue my vision, which would no doubt be a challenging path, yet I would be happy. You guessed it; after discussing the options with my wife, I choose happiness over wealth. One cannot ever celebrate if they are not truly happy on the inside.

> "Nowadays true job satisfaction and happiness is about fulfilling your full potential, tapping into your own creativity and feeling that you can make a difference."
>
> -Chris Humphries

Listen carefully; I am not stating that you should quit your job tomorrow. We must be wise about our decisions, as for me I carefully planned my departure from the workplace. One must consider his or her family and lifestyle when making a decision such as this. Everything takes time, so take your time and plan. But do follow your dreams, visions, and goals because at the end when it is completed there will be a time to celebrate your accomplishments.

I believe all the strength that we need to accomplish our visions successfully is already within us. And that it was placed in us by Christ since the beginning. We must trust in Christ and believe in ourselves to see it through. There is an end to our road, and the road will not always be uphill. So, stick to it, pursue it and rest in vision.

Hebrews 3:16-19 KJV:

16. For some, when they had heard, did provoke: howbeit not all that come out of Egypt by Moses. **17.** But with whom was he grieved forty-years? Was it not with them that had sinned, whose carcasses fell in the wilderness? **18.** And to whom sware he that they should not enter into his rest, but to them that believe not? **19.** So we see that they could not enter in because of unbelief.

Hebrews 4:1-4 KJV:

1. Let us therefore fear, lest, a promise being left us of entering into his rest, any of you should seem to come short of it. **2.** For to us was the gospel preached, as well as to them: but the word preached did not profit them, not being mixed with faith in them that heard it. **3.** For we which have believed do enter into rest, as he said. As I have sworn in my wrath, if they shall enter into my rest: although the works were finished from the foundation of the world. **4.** For he spake in a certain place of the seventh day on this wise, And God did rest the seventh day from all his works.

> *"Laziness may appear attractive, but work gives satisfaction."*
>
> *-Anne Frank*

From the two above passages, one can come to the understanding that the Lord wants us to enter into His rest. But the writer of Hebrews takes this notion of rest event further by stating, one must believe in order to enter into that rest. The writer explains this process of entering God's rest by first giving a snapshot of the story of the Israelites being led through the wilderness by Moses. And according to **Hebrews 3:19**, those who did not believe were left to die in that same wilderness, never to experience the rest beyond.

Now let us step back and examine this further, because any reader would clearly identify that the writer of Hebrews is referring to the exodus from Egypt and the journey to the promise land.[1] Yet, when writing the author does not refer to it as the promise land, but calls it the rest of God. Therefore, entering the promise land/promises of God, is the same as entering the rest of God. Meaning the only way we can experience rest in life, is by entering into the promise land of rest. However, the only means of entering this rest in God, is by belief in His word. And by believing in the gospel being preached to us by God's Spirit and that by His massagers.

Many of us in the body and those outside the body, have yet to find rest and peace in life due to the fact we have not believed in the promises of God's word. God does not change, and being that He does not change, His uses the same method He used to guide the Israelites to the promise land to guide us into our promise. This method is His word, a word which has been preached since the foundation of the world, and this word tells us to believe what He says.

Before we go any further, let me list and go over a few definitions of words taken from **Hebrews 4:1-3**. Afterwards, I will insert those definitions back into the passage for a clearer understanding of the writer's thoughts.

- verse 1 <u>fear</u> = Greek *phobeo* = to frighten, to be alarmed, revere.[2]
- verse 1 <u>promise</u> = Greek *epangelia* = an announcement, information, pledge, a divine assurance of good.[3]
- verse 1 <u>being left</u> = to abandon.[4]
- verse 1 <u>rest</u> = abode.[5]

---

[1] see **Exodus 3:7-8**
[2] see Strgs#5399
[3] see Strgs#1860
[4] see Strgs#2641
[5] see Strgs#2663

- verse 2 <u>preached</u> = Greek *evangelizo* = to announce good news.[1]
- verse 2 (2nd) <u>preached</u> = Greek *akoe* = hearing, the thing heard.[2]
- verse 2 <u>profit</u> = Greek *opheleo* = to benefit.[3]
- verse 2 <u>mixed</u> = to commingle, to combine or assimilate.[4]
- verse 2 <u>faith</u> = Greek *pistis* = persuasion, credence, moral conviction (of religious truth, or the truthfulness of God or a religious teacher).[5]
- verse 3 <u>wrath</u> = Greek *orgē* = desire (as a reaching forth or excitement of the mind), violent passion, punishment.[6]
- verse 4 <u>rest</u> = Greek *katapauō* = to settle down, to colonize, to cause to desist.[7]
- verse 4 <u>from</u> = Greek apo = off, separation, departure, cessation, completion, reversal, out of.[8]

I know that was much, but I believe them to be necessary to truly understand what the writer is attempted to get across. Now let us insert those definitions into the passage.

Hebrews 4:1-4 KJV: with definitions

---

[1] see Strgs#2641
[2] see Strgs#189
[3] see Strgs#5623
[4] see Strgs#4786
[5] see Strgs#4102
[6] see Strgs#4102
[7] see Strgs#2664
[8] see Strgs#575

1. Let us therefore <u>be alarmed</u>, lest, a <u>divine assurance of good</u> abandon us of entering into his <u>abode</u>, any of you should seem to come short of it. **2.** For unto us was the gospel <u>of good news announced</u>, as well as unto them: but word <u>of hearing</u> did not benefit them, not commingling with <u>the truthfulness of God</u> in them that heard it. **3.** For we which have believed do enter into rest, as he said, As I have sworn in my <u>passion</u>, if they shall enter into my rest: although the works were finished from the foundation of the world. **4.** For he spake in a certain place of the seventh day on this wise, And God did <u>colonize</u> the seventh day <u>out of</u> all his works.

We can read from this simple translation, how God wanted His creation to enter into the promise of His rest. He has been proclaiming and preaching to the world, *"Come on in, in me there is all you will ever need. There is life, they is joy, there is profitability, and there is rest. And all you have to do is believe that what I have spoken into your life to be true."* In order to abode in our Lord or to abode in our promise land, we must both allow His truthful word and our hearing of it to work together for our benefit. We cannot afford to have one without the other, *"Let us therefore be alarmed, lest, a divine assurance of good abandon us of entering into his abode."*

Unbelief not only causes us not to experience the promise of rest in God. It also causes us to wander through our life purposefulness, until we feel our life becoming a carcass. Carcasses in **Hebrews 3:17**, is the Greek word *kolon*, and it is defined as a limb of the body as if lopped off.[1] Therefore, being out of His rest/promise is as if members of our body are being lopped off. In other words, our life begins to fall spiritually apart.

---

[1] see Strgs#2966

If we desire to enter into the rest of His promise for our life, as much as God desires it. It is from the place of rest and promise that we are to do the work the Lord requires of us, regarding ourselves and others. We can no longer be unbelieving believers. You may be asking, "What is an unbelieving-believer?" Well, an unbelieving-believer, is someone who believes in Jesus being their Lord and Savior, but do not believe in the truthfulness of all God says about them. Such as God saying, "I will deliver you from alcoholism, or I love you, or I will bring about your purpose in life." Much of the body of believers believes in Christ, yet, much of the body fail to do or perform what He has asked us to do for others and for ourselves. Once again you may be asking, "How can I say or know this?" I know this because it has been happening since biblical times.

James 1:22-25 KJV:

22. But be ye doers of the word, and not hearers only, deceiving your own selves. **23.** For if any be a hearer of the word, and not a doer, he is like unto a man beholding his natural face in a glass: **24.** For he beholdeth himself and goeth his way, and straightway forgetteth what manner of man he was. **25.** But whoso looketh into the perfect law of liberty, and continueth therein, he being not a forgetful hearer, but a doer of the work, this man shall be blessed in his deed.

Since the time of James, God has been telling His church. Not only should we hear the word, but also to become doers of that which we have heard. Being a hearer only, simply leads us to deceiving ourselves. How, with false narrations of the mind. Therefore, we should no longer be hearing we can enter His rest only. For it is now the time that we enter that rest by doing what He has instructed.

<u>Doer</u> is the Greek word *poiētēs* and it defined as a performer or poet. [1] It was used by individuals such as Xenophon, a Greek military strategist and Plato, the philosopher, to denote a maker, producer, performer, and author. So, in essence, to be a doer ultimately means someone who write what was spoken, bring it into manifestation. Or someone who acts out exactly what has been spoken.

We must not become the individual who looks into the mirror, and forgets their worth after leaving it. I say worth, because the Lord describes each of us as being valuable and precious as a pearl.[2] When standing in front the mirror (God's word), we believe what we see or what God says about us, because the evidence of our worth is in front our eyes. Yet, when the evidence of our appearance is no longer visible, we no longer trust what was said. And begin to toss our value into the world, as though it is meaningless. In this state, we believe what the world says about us and what it says we can accomplish over God's word.

However, the fact remains, we must not cast the value/promise of ourselves out into the world to be trampled.[3] Whether in front the mirror or not, we must believe in the value of ourselves and what we can accomplish. We must write out and author the promises of God in our lives. By becoming doers, performers, and produces to our life. With God's aid, we write out our lives, not the world.

If God calls you to be a parent, walk and act as a parent should. If He call you to the ministry, prepare your life to minister by spending time with the Father through study, worship, and prayer. If He calls you to the world of business, prepare yourself for the journey by taking the necessary steps

---

[1] see Strgs#4163
[2] see **Matthew 13:44-46**
[3] see **Matthew 7:6**

to learn the trade. Then and only then, can we enter His rest and our purpose.

Conclusion

With all that has been mentioned throughout the book, I would like to take a moment to bring out one last point which is, how vital that we walk in our purpose and do all that is necessary to be successful at it. We as Christians must learn and discern opportunities of success, in order to be able to take advantages that present itself. Success is not necessarily about how much we reap from our labor but more of how effectively we seize and utilize the window of opportunity when it arises.

To truly grasp the concept of seizing the moment, we need to examine the moment in history when Christ entered the world. You see, God brought Christ into the world at His perfect time when it was purposed for Him to arrive in c.3BC. He brought Christ into the world after the Romans had fought one of their bloodiest civil wars. The victor, Octavius, later Emperor Augustus, then established his *Pax Romana* (Roman Peace), and because of the peace, individuals were able to travel throughout the empire in relative safety.

With the Roman Empire at peace under Emperor Augustus, there was a boom in Rome's infrastructure, specifically roads and ports. Roman naval ships patrolled waters, protecting Rome's interest. Being that Rome depended heavily upon imports from its subordinates to survive, the emperor made sure it was a priority to travel safely.

The safety in traversing the empire ultimately made it easier for the apostles to conduct their missionary work. Now Paul the Apostle has been noted for helping to lead the charge of Christianity. To do that, he had to be purpose-driven, believing that nothing could hinder his work in the Lord. He trusted in the Lord, and by putting his trust in the Lord, he helped to spread the gospel in Europe and eventually the world through the Europeans.

You see, the opportunity of a successful salvation through Christ came long before Paul. However, Paul was able to see what the Lord was doing in his life, along with recognizing the usefulness of the Roman road that networked the Empire together. If he did not use the roads that were created by the Romans, the gospels might not have been as successful at reaching as many people as he did. He saw the opportunity of using the Roman roads and used them. The Roman roads were so successful at networking the empire, that the historian/Roman Elite, Tacticius complained about how it allowed so-called filth from the far ends of the empire to make its way to Rome and pollute it.

Romans 8:30 reads, *"Moreover whom he did predestinate, then he also called! And whom he called, then he also justified:, and whom he justified, then he also glorified,"* KJV.

I believe we are all called by the Father, and with His calling, He has predestined us all to be successful at various things. It is our attitude toward Him and ourselves that hinder humanity. Being predestined and purpose driven to success by God, He will and can grant us a time of peace. A time of peace that allows us to take notice of the roads of opportunity laid out before us. Knowing that through it all, it is by Christ's purpose that we are successful. He has predestined us in a time such as now to walk the roads of life and spread His words of salvation through the talents He has bestowed upon us. Be motivated and determined to complete your task successfully.

Keeping in mind that what we desire or want may not come overnight or may never come, even in knowing that we must know that God is sovereign, and He answers to no one but Himself. We must be mindful that we do not attempt to force God to do our bidding. He is our Father, He hears us and wants the best for us. According to **Ecclesiastes 3:1-15** everything has a time and season, so prep yourself now for when your time and season approaches. Do not be like the foolish virgins in **Matthew 25:1-13** and wait for the last minute to prepare yourself.

Times will be hard when walking towards our goals and visions; sometimes it may even appear that we are not accomplishing much. Yet I say, that if you see the vision and push toward that vision while keeping Christ as the focal point, success will be your outcome. For joy is not in wealth but witnessing the change of one's life by Christ, even if that life is your own.

The Seven Principles of Success are not meant for chasing wealth and finances. These principles are for building up the Church of Christ, within our homes, children, marriages, schooling, occupations or ministry, if it is applied to all that the church does. The Lord wants His people to be successful in all aspects, not just with finances. **Matthew 6:24** reads, *"We cannot serve God and Mammon."* "Serve" is defined as "to be a slave to."[1] "Mammon" is defined as "wealth personified, riches, treasure."[2]

The purpose of this book was not written to get the church to chase after Mammon or riches. It was written to build up the confidence of God's people, making them aware that the Father encourages us to be successful in all aspects of our lives, not only with our finances. We are not made to serve riches but the Lord of Heaven. *"But seek ye first the Kingdom of God, and his righteousness, and all these things shall be added unto you."*[3] Seek out the Lord first and all that He has for you will be added to you.

_____

[1] see Strgs#1398
[2] see Strgs#3126
[3] see **Matthew 6:33**

Seven Biblical Principals of Success

Day 1 – Let the light of your vision shine: Be inspired to do something new.

Day 2 – Separate your vision from the darkness: Join to those that believe in you.

Day 3 – Give life to your vision: Began working towards your vision.

Day 4 – Guide and Steer your vision: Be the leader of your vision.

Day 5 – Multiply your vision: Begin increasing your vision's productivity.

Day 6 – Be dominant over your vision: Know your field of study or area of work.

Day 7 – Rest in your vision: Take peace in what you have accomplished.

Bonus Chapter
Promises of the Lord

Exodus 3:7-9 KJV:

7. And the Lord said, I have surely seen[1] the affliction of my people which are in Egypt, and have heard[2] their cry[3] by reason of their taskmasters; for I know their sorrows[4]; **8.** And I am come down to deliverer them out of the hand of the Egyptians, and to bring them up out of that land unto a good land and a large, unto a land flowing with milk and honey; unto the place of the Canaanites, and the Hittites, and the Amorites, and the Perizzites, and the Hivites, and Jebusites. **9.** Now therefore, behold, the cry of the children of Israel is come unto me: and I have also seen the oppression wherewith the Egyptians oppress them.

Being believers of Christ, we must know that He sees and hears our cries, and He understands our sorrows. Everything that we go through, the Lord is near to us and for this reason He is our deliverer. By lifting our eyes to Him, He can and will deliver us from the land of Egypt (bondage) and into a land flowing with milk and honey (The Promised Land).

Nehemiah 9:15 KJV:

---

[1] seen = sight of others, stare, consider, to be near [Strgs#7200]
[2] heard = to publish, report, call together, diligently, discern, obedient, proclaim [Strgs#8085]
[3] cry = to proclaim, distress [literally emotions]
[4] sorrows = grieving, have pain, make sad [Strgs#3510]

15. And gave them bread from Heaven for their hunger, and brought forth water for them out of the rock for their thirst, and <u>promised</u> them that they should <u>go in</u> to possess the land which you had sworn to give them.

Nehemiah 9:15, and the verses before and after it, was an oral history of what the Israelites went through during the Exodus. And Nehemiah with his words was both honoring God for what he had done for his people, while yet reminding the people to keep their faith in the Lord and remember what He had done for them already. When studying **Nehemiah 9:15** I found it to be the most memorable verse out of the chapter. It was as if the Lord had opened another door, showing me how I should live or view this Christian walk of ours.

- Go in = besiege, bring to pass, <u>eat</u>, <u>employ</u>, go down to war, <u>grant</u>
- Promised in **Nehemiah 9:15** is the same Hebrew word for said in **Genesis 1:3**, which states, *"And God said, let there be light."* Promised is the Hebrew word *'âmar*, and it is defined as to say, answer, appoint, avouch, bid, boast self, charge, determine, publish and challenge [Strongs#559].

The scripture describes how the Lord talks in different ways, such as in a whisper or loud thundering. However, the power in His voice or the authority of His words remain the same. No matter how He says it, His power and authority remain the same. If God says it, it must be, no matter how it is delivered.

So, when God said let there be light, the light manifested immediately because of the authority in his voice. This also applies with God's promises to man-kind and the church. From the very moment He makes a promise, it is manifested. His promises are instantaneous. However, just as with the Hebrews were promised the lands flowing with milk and honey and had to take a journey to it, so likewise it is our task to reach our promise.[1]

Our promises can either take a few days or forty years. The Hebrews journey from Egypt to the Promise land was only 300 miles which could have been traveled in just over forty days; instead, it took them over 3,000 miles and forty years to make it. In other words, our faith and attitude towards God determine how fast we reach that promise.

The fact remains that we are the only ones that can hinder ourselves from reaching the promises spoken over us. Whatever the Lord has spoken to you, it already out there for you to reach, you just have to make the necessary steps to get there. And if the Lord says it is out there, then it is out there. And it will remain out there until the day you die. Although one generation was disobedient towards Him, God did not go back on His word. The Lord allowed a span of forty years to pass, that is forty years that the older generation could have used to repent of their ways then enter the Promised Land. But by remaining hardened of neck, God allowed their time to pass, until that entire generation of stiff neck people had died out; then passed their inheritance to their children. You see, once God promises something, He does not give it to another. If the promise goes unfulfilled, then it can pass to another.

We must take the Lord's promises towards us and run with them, allowing nothing to lead us astray, remaining strong and courageous through this journey to the Promised Land. **Exodus 14** speaks of how the Hebrews stop at the sea shore when Pharaoh was chasing them. The Hebrews had to see the sea from a distance as they approached it, knowing that crossing it would be nearly impossible, for they had no ships. Yet they continued to walk towards it, having faith that

---

[1] See **Exodus 3:1-8, 16:35, 17:3-6**

their God would make a way. Why, because He promised to bring them to a land flowing with milk in honey. Yes, they murmured towards God and their leader, yet they continued to walk towards the vast sea before them.

Now how many of us are guilty of looking at the vast sea ahead of us, and because discouraged then turn around in fear of failing to cross it? Many of us, and I have to admit that I am one of them. But we must remember that it is not our job to make a way, it is God's. As He is the Promise, He is the Way, He is the Truth and He is the Life. **Titus 1:2** states that God cannot lie. The promises that He has for us, are for us even if we never reach it. It remains ours until we die. In other words, at the point of death we are released from the promise, at which point the promises goes to the next generation.

God has so much faith in His ability to help us reach our promises, that He puts resources into place to help aid us along the way. Even if our progress towards the promise takes forty years, He will supply food[1] (the word- **Matthew 26:26**), water[2] (life- **John 7:38**) and clothing[3] (comfort- **John 14:26**)

And through our walk we must remind and repeat to ourselves of that which the Lord has for us. Because when we forget, we as a people tend to work less to reach that promise. Out of sight out of mind. God is the opposite, as He often and frequently reminded the Israel of all He had done for them, that they might work diligently at becoming a holy nation.

Even hundreds of years after Moses, God was still reminding His people of how He keeps His promises. **Romans 15:8** reads, *"Now I say that Jesus Christ was a minister of*

---

[1] compare **Exodus 16:35**

[2] compare **Exodus 17:3-6**

[3] compare **Deuteronomy 8:4, 29:5**

circumcision for the truth of God, to confirm the promises[1] made unto the fathers," KJV.

"Fathers" here speaks of the founding fathers of the Hebrews. So, promises made to Abraham were fulfilled by Jesus. Promises made to Israel were fulfilled by Jesus. Promises made to you are fulfilled by Jesus.

- Our Lord said, "Ask[2] and it shall be given you; seek, and ye shall find; knock and it shall be opened unto you," KJV.[3]

Being believers, we must ask the Lord concerning our desires or that which we crave to have. And we ask by seeking. Not that of seeking after our desires but seeking after our Lord. For the word "seek" is defined as *"to worship God*, to enquire and require."[4] Seeking the Lord, we learn of the requirement needed to reach our promises. In worship our spirits enquire from the Lord a sense of direction. Through worship we learn if our own desires are right for us. We learn if they line up with the Lord's plan for our life.

Worship makes us aware of how to achieve. As the word "find" is defined as "perceive".[5] Once we gained the ability to perceive we can begin to knock on doors of opportunity, and by enquiring of the Lord in worship, those doors of opportunity are required to open for us.

- "Open" comes from a Greek root word meaning everyman. When you are in constant worship with

---

[1] promises- an announcement, pledge, and divine assurance of good [Strgs#1860]
[2] ask – crave, call for, desire [Strgs#1547]
[3] **Matthew 7:7**
[4] see Strgs#2212
[5] See Strgs#2147

God, everyman/people must present you opportunities to aid you with reaching your promises.

Christ was and is a sign from God, that no matter how long it may take, our Heavenly Father keeps His promises. We as a body must record and maintain all that is spoken over us, that we may refer back and say, "Lord it is written here that you spoke good things over me." We must speak and reach after our promises, as they will not come forth if we do not pursue towards them.

By the Lord believing in us, we therefore must believe in ourselves; which fits another definition for "promise," determined. And if we put this into perspective, we learn that the Lord is determined to bring all His promises to pass. Not only does He believe, but He is determined.

The body has yet to grasp what it truly means to be a son and daughter. The scripture reads, "And I will be a Father to you, and you will be my sons and daughters, say the Lord Almighty," NIV.[1] "Will be" comes from the Greek root word *eimi*, i-mee, meaning "*I exist.*"[2] We as a people exist because the Lord desires to have sons and daughters to speak well over. We exist so that the Father may speak promises over us, entitling us to His eternal riches. We exist to seek the Lord in worship and to have His favor, for all that He says to us is a promise.

---

[1] **2 Cor. 6:18**
[2] see Strgs#1510

Success by Tiffany Gibbs

What does success mean to you?
Is it the accomplishing of goals?
Is it making dreams come true?
For some, success is just surviving
Then moving past the day to day onward to thriving
Others only seek to get past the emptiness they feel searching
through their fellow man then looking to God,
To heal
Success can be found in a happy home
Rejoicing in the breaking of generational curses
Symbolized by a family of your own
Growing, moving onward
Pursuing and achieving goals
Seeing life differently
Grasping the possibilities
The faith to see past what is currently seen
A new life
A new start
A healthy relationship
Success is knowing the latter can
Always be better than the former part

"Moreover the profit of the earth is for all,"
Ecclesiastes 5:9

OTHER WORKS FROM DAMEON GIBBS

- *The World Around Them: Commentaries of An Early 20ᵗʰ Century School Teacher*
- *The Seven Days of God*
- *The Anointed One: Words That Became Living Flesh*
- *The Walls of Jerusalem vols. 1*
- *The Molding*
- *Wounds of Salvation*
- *Jesus You Are*

Coming Soon:

- Found in the Storm
- The Walls of Jerusalem vol. 2

Other Works from Crown of Glory Ministries

- *The Numbers of God* by Donald Peart
- *The Completions of the Ages* by Donald Peart
- *Sex Pleasures* by Donald Peart
- *The Many False Prophets: The Tail of the Dragon* by Donald Peart
- *The Completion of The Ages by Donald Peart*
- *The Last Hour* by Donald Peart
- *Vision Real* by Donald Peart
- *The Days of the 7ᵗʰ Angel* by Donald Peart
- *Forgiven 490* by Donald Peart
- *The Torah: The Principle of Giving* by Donald Peart
- *Examining Doctrine* by Donald Peart
- *The False Prophet: Alias Another Beast* by Donald Peart
- *The Beast* by Donald Peart
- *The Lamb* by Donald Peart
- *The Work of Lawlessness Revealed* by Donald Peart
- *Son of Man: Prophesy Against the False Prophet and Cast Him Down* by Donald Peart
- *The Time Came* by Donald Peart

- *Jesus' Resurrection: Our Inheritance* by Donald Peart
- *Exousia: Your God Given Authority* by Donald Peart
- *When the Lord Made the Tempter* by Donald Peart
- *Poiema* by Judith Peart
- *Wisdom From Above* by Judith Peart
- *100 Nevers* by Judith Peart
- *Sexual Healing* by Judith Peart
- *My Life Is An Open Book* by Tiffany Gibbs
- *Words to my God* by Tiffany Gibbs
- *The Lord Is My Light* by Tiffany Gibbs
- *The Moon Is A Piece Of Swiss Cheese In The Sky by Tiffany Gibbs*

Notes:

www.ingramcontent.com/pod-product-compliance
Lightning Source LLC
Chambersburg PA
CBHW051220120626
46547CB00013B/1444